PRAYER DID IT!

PRAYER DID IT!

A 21st Century Miracle

Patti Janacaro

iUniverse, Inc.
Bloomington

Prayer Did It!
A 21st Century Miracle

iUniverse books may be ordered through booksellers or by contacting:

iUniverse
1663 Liberty Drive
Bloomington, IN 47403
www.iuniverse.com
1-800-Authors (1-800-288-4677)

Because of the dynamic nature of the Internet, any web addresses or links contained in this book may have changed since publication and may no longer be valid. The views expressed in this work are solely those of the author and do not necessarily reflect the views of the publisher, and the publisher hereby disclaims any responsibility for them.

Any people depicted in stock imagery provided by Thinkstock are models, and such images are being used for illustrative purposes only.

Certain stock imagery © Thinkstock.

ISBN: 978-1-4502-8905-4 (sc)
ISBN: 978-1-4502-8906-1 (ebk)

Printed in the United States of America

iUniverse rev. date: 02/03/2011

This is dedicated to all of our wonderful friends who, through their continuous prayers, overwhelming love, and support, have pulled us through this most difficult time in our lives. There are too many of you to list, but you know who you are.

Thank you!
Thank you!
Thank you!

A special thanks to Cathy Newton, my longtime friend and three-time-published author. You encouraged me, believed in me, and coached me. Cathy, you really are the best. Thank you!

A miracle is an event that creates faith. That is the purpose and nature of miracles. Frauds deceive an event that creates faith does not deceive; therefore it is not a fraud, but a miracle.

—George Bernard Shaw

INTRODUCTION

Miracles still happen in today's world. We have witnessed one in our lives, and I have felt compelled to write this story to encourage others to never give up hope.

Our miracle happened on April 2, 2006. When we were experiencing the bleakest hour, the power of prayer shone through, and the glory of God blinded us with the shining light of his love. "This is God's work," the doctor said. "This is a miracle."

This ordeal took place during Lent of 2006. It all started on Fat Tuesday and was completed by Easter Sunday. The power of prayer by so many people and of so many denominations all over the world was the key to this miracle. Because of this miracle, I felt I had to tell the story about what we had witnessed.

It is very humbling to be the recipient of a miracle of this magnitude. We as family members feel like we had received this miracle as much as Larry had. When people were dying every second, we had to wonder why we were the lucky ones.

So many of our friends have told us that they had gotten away from praying until this had happened to Larry, but they are now praying again. Maybe that is why this happened: to bring people back to God and prayers.

Whatever the reason, we thank you, God, for sparing Larry. I'm sure his work here on earth is not yet finished.

We prayed, and you listened.

"Medically speaking, this should not have, could not have happened," my husband's primary physician told us. "There is no medical explanation for it. This is God's work. This is a miracle." We just stared at him as he continued. "Everything is returning to normal. His kidney is almost back to normal. His white blood cells are back. Temperature is normal, and infections are gone. This is unheard of. This just does not happen."

It was Monday morning, April 3, 2006, at 9:00 AM. We were at a scheduled family meeting with my husband's doctor. The meeting had been scheduled to decide if we should take Larry off life support. Every major organ, except his heart, was shutting down, and he had no white blood cells to fight off infections.

Now, his doctor was telling us that he would be okay! He was going to make it! We kept waiting for the "other shoe to drop," but it never did. "This truly is a miracle," he told us. That happened on Sunday, April 2, after more than four weeks in the cardiac intensive care unit of the North Kansas City Hospital in Kansas City, Missouri.

PROLOGUE

L arry objected when the nurse asked him to remove the three medals he wore on a chain around his neck. Soon after he lost that battle, Larry handed the medals to me for safekeeping. I put them around my own neck. It was standing policy to remove all jewelry before surgery, and I felt it best to keep them with me so I could give them back as soon as he was released from the hospital. The three medals were a scapular, a Saint Peraquin (the patron saint for cancer patients), and the miraculous medal.

Three days after the successful removal of a malignant tumor on my husband's one remaining kidney, the other being removed seven years earlier for the same reason, I was fingering those medals in a state of total confusion.

The three of us, my daughter, my son, and me, had just received an emergency call from the hospital at 5:45 AM on the morning of March 3. My husband, their father, had just been transferred to the cardiac intensive care unit. We were not allowed in the room, because the doctors, nurses, and machines were working to save his life. After Larry was stabilized, we were told that the next forty-eight hours would be the most critical.

We were so afraid and so confused as we watched Larry fade into a coma. I felt faint, and a nurse got me a glass of water. The three of us just waited for some news or some explanation. We were all trying to be strong for each other.

Our daughter, Annette, an elementary school teacher with a husband and two young daughters, had rushed to the hospital after she had arranged for a substitute teacher. Our son, Joe, with a wife and two young children, had just started his insurance agency two months earlier. Earlier that day, he had made the call to his office to inform his staff of the situation. Somehow, both of our children, even with such busy careers, managed to come to the hospital each day and spend hours on the end standing by their dad as the weeks and months rolled on. We all knew that Larry would have done the same despite his busy banker's schedule.

Larry, the large, handsome man with the big heart, the teddy bear that loved everyone, knew no strangers and devoted so much of his time to charitable organizations just so that he could help someone, was now in trouble.

Every morning and every night, Larry had always prayed for so many people, and he attended daily mass as often as possible. Now, *he* desperately needed the prayers.

The three of us started praying, and it did not take long for the word to spread. Larry's prayer chains started up and kept going for two and a half months. Each day, more and more people started praying. The number of prayers from around the world coming in was absolutely amazing, and the number kept growing.

The significance of Larry's medals should not be overlooked—scapular, cancer, miraculous! Wow!

This kind, good man certainly had the prayer corner covered, and something magnificent occurred. We should never underestimate the power of the prayer.

God loves all of us, and he gets us through the hard times either by walking with us or by carrying us when we need him the most. We have firsthand proof of this, and this is what happened. Everyone has a story, and this is ours.

Our Miracle

We witnessed a miracle
It was oh, so grand.
We were all there together
And saw it firsthand.

We were all crying as our loved one was dying
But we never gave up as we
Prayed 'round the bed where
Our family's rock was lying.

Yes, we were praying like a marathon band
Surely not expecting it when God showed His hand,
Now we want to shout it all over this land.

How do you thank Him when He has so much to do
And He takes the time to focus on you?
So we will tell our story for the world to know too,
We believe in Him. Seeing this, wouldn't you?

CONTENTS

CHAPTER 1

THE SURGERY

After my husband lost his right kidney to cancer in 1999, I knew that Larry was very apprehensive when his urologist told him on February 1, 2006, that a spot on his left kidney needed to be removed. He was facing another surgery.

I began to sense that Larry was having bad feelings about another surgery by some of the things he was saying and doing during the four weeks prior to his surgery. I found out later that several people had also sensed that. Larry obviously felt that something would not go well with this surgery, which was scheduled for February 28, 2006.

However, the surgery went very well. The malignant tumor was removed, and he was recovering well. The prognosis was good. The doctor was pleased. Larry was walking down the hallways several times a day, sitting in the chair, and planning to go home in a few days. Unfortunately, that would not happen for another nine and a half weeks.

I felt uneasy as I left the hospital on Thursday night at around 10:30 PM, because Larry had been feeling nauseous all day. His doctor had given him medication for the nausea, but Larry was afraid of developing a post-op illness as he had after his last kidney surgery. As it turned out, he was indeed developing another, and he was feeling bad. His nurse told me that she would call me if anything changed, so I headed home to get some rest. I was worried about Larry, so I called his nurse at around 12:30 AM to check on him. The nurse told me that he had had an incident earlier and that he had vomited but that he was doing fine now.

"Oh! Should I come back down to the hospital?" I asked.

She told me that was not necessary. They were watching him, and they would call me if there was any change.

I wish I had followed my instincts and gone back. Oh, how I wish that I had.

Five hours later, the nurse called back and told me that they were transferring Larry to the cardiac intensive care unit. She told me to hurry but to be careful. We did not know until later that Larry had coded that morning, Friday March 3, 2006.

As I burst through the door of the CICU, they could immediately tell who I was, because a nurse quickly ushered me to room 929. We had no idea that this would be our home for approximately the next seven weeks.

You pray in your distress and in your need;
would that you might pray also in the fullness of
your joy and in your days of abundance.
—Kahlil Gibran, the prophet

CHAPTER 2

THE DARK DAYS

Room 929 was full of doctors and nurses working on my fifty-six-year-old high-school sweetheart and husband of more than thirty-five years. A respirator tube was being inserted, and several machines were being hooked up. Everyone was rushing around, and I was told to wait outside in the hallway until they were finished.

Because Larry had not gone into the drug-induced coma, he was still awake. Finally, I was allowed to enter the room. He was staring into my eyes and moving his lips, but he could not speak out loud because of the respirator tube. He was trying so hard to tell me something. I'll never forget the look in his eyes. I was so tortured by the look and because I would not be able to ask him what he had been trying to say for six and a half weeks as he slipped into the coma. When I asked him later, he could not remember, so we'll never know for sure.

My daughter, Annette, my son, Joe, and I had so many questions we needed answered. What had happened? What was wrong? How serious was it? What was his condition? We knew something was very wrong, but we did not know yet that Larry was critically ill.

Back in his other hospital room, Larry aspirated his vomit. When this happened, he swallowed hydrochloric acid straight into his lungs. The acid burned and paralyzed 90 percent of his lungs, causing a condition called acute respiratory distress syndrome (ARDS), one of the worst lung conditions. Fifty percent of patients with ARDS did not survive. The next forty-eight hours would be the most critical. Larry could die. If he didn't die, he would have a very long road ahead of him.

Larry's primary doctor had known Larry since high school, so he knew that my husband was strong and would be fighting for his life. Larry loved life too much not to fight. The doctor also knew that his patient's lungs, partial kidney, and heart were all stressing each other and that only time would tell.

My daughter, son, and I struggled to grasp all that had happened. Just one night prior, their father and my husband had been fine, recovering from a successful surgery, but now, there was a good chance he would die. We couldn't lose him. We just couldn't. We knew he wanted to live. We would do anything and everything to keep him here. We counted twelve tubes plus the respirator that were hooked up to him that morning as Larry lay so still in a coma. We listened as the nurse patiently tried to explain these devices to us and what they were designed to do.

The CICU waiting room began to fill up after friends and family had heard the news of what had happened. We all camped out after each selected a spot and tried to make some sense out of what the doctors were telling us.

At this point, Larry had several groups of doctors in addition to his primary physician. Cancer doctors, kidney doctors, cardiologists, pulmonary doctors, urologists, gastroenterologists, anesthesiologists, general surgeons, radiologists, and respiratory therapists were all working together as Larry lay in a coma, unaware that anything had happened. He would never remember any of these experiences, because one of the drugs would cause amnesia, which really was a blessing in the end. As the doctors constantly filed into the room and checked on Larry, they were all very kind and explained his condition to us as best they could.

We all began to pray in our own way as we sat and held his hand, wiped his brow, or just simply stared at him. This was all so surreal.

Larry was anointed for the first of five times on Friday afternoon of March 3, when he was lying in the CICU.

By Saturday, things were getting worse. A SWAN device that measures the fluid around the heart was inserted into his neck. More tubes were hooked up, and all of the doctors looked even grimmer than they had yesterday after they had examined him.

I did not realize just how serious his condition was until one of the doctors asked me if I knew how he felt about life support. I did know, because we had discussed it. I was stunned by the question, and suddenly, I was very afraid. I began to cry. It was a valid question, I now know, but it made me realize that we might have to make some very difficult decisions in the near future.

Friends began arriving with baskets of food and prayed the rosary with us in the waiting room. Their support and concern was so very comforting to all of us. They remained with us throughout the night of March 4 as Larry coded three times. It was a rough night. Katie, the night nurse, brought him back three times, which was unbelievable, because only 5 percent of all code-blue patients survived and Larry had survived four code blues by now. We began calling Katie our "angel nurse."

The pulmonary doctor was in the room the first time he crashed. Several nurses came rushing in as all the machines beeped and went crazy. They left the cart in the room just in case it happened again. And it did.

Annette had been in the room the second time it had happened, and I had been in the room the third and final time he had coded.

It was such a helpless feeling, knowing we could lose him at any time and not knowing what we could do to help him.

Maybe it was the rosary made of rose petals and blessed by the Pope that we had placed in Larry's hand at around 1:00 AM on Sunday morning that was responsible for his stabilization. It could have been all the prayers being said in the waiting room, too, but I really thought it was the combination. Whichever it was, Katie said she felt relieved around three o'clock in the morning, and she felt that Larry was going to make it.

None of us had given up throughout the night, and as we discussed with Katie the fact that, we really believed that the glass was half-full, not half-empty. Katie said that she felt the same way. Maybe our hope had been what had kept him alive that night. Nonetheless, we never gave up, and Larry started to improve.

We were told that if his condition stayed the same or took baby steps forward, that would be good. If he took baby steps backward, however, his prognosis would worsen.

The next week and a half proved to be good in signs of improvement. Very early each morning, he was wheeled downstairs for a chest X-ray that the doctors would compare to the one taken the day before. He was making great progress, although it was a very slow recovery, too.

March 15 was the first day they attempted to take Larry off of the respirator. He had been on the respirator for more than two weeks by then, and that was the maximum time allotted, because the risk of infection increased after that. Larry stayed off the respirator for about forty minutes but then started struggling for air. His lungs were not clear enough yet, so the tube was reinserted.

Less than a week later, there was no choice but to perform a tracheotomy and remove the tube, as infection was imminent. A second attempt to get Larry off the respirator also failed. Larry needed the tracheotomy, because he could not breathe on his own yet. Although he remained in a coma, he was getting better.

During the next three weeks, Larry remained in the CICU. It seemed that each day ran into the next. Although it was dark and ominous in that unit, we definitely felt much love and compassion from the nurses and other personnel. Each day, we would grieve for other families as they lost loved ones. We also saw so many survive like our Larry.

One of the nurses and I decided that this unit of the hospital was like purgatory—an abyss, an in-between place, a place to hover between life and death, a holding place between heaven and hell. While I was growing up, I was taught that the prayers of the faithful would deliver the souls in purgatory from their abyss. With enough prayers, they would eventually be able to enter into heaven. This was what was happening to

Larry. The prayers of so many people all over the world were working! He was "out of the woods" now. He would soon be moving out to the intensive care unit and into a step-down room. There was a light at the end of the tunnel now. The nightmare was almost over. The prayers of faithful friends were working!

We had come full circle when the roller coaster we were riding took the biggest dip of all. All of Larry's major organs, except his heart, began shutting down. Infection spread throughout his bloodstream, kidney, and bladder. An infectious disease doctor was called in, and several antibiotics were administered. They began dialysis, but they eventually had to stop treatment because of all the infections running through his body. Now he had zero white blood cells to fight off infections, because one of the antibiotics had wiped out all of them. He was given Nuprogen, a drug that helped produce white blood cells, but if he did not produce them in three days, his chances of survival were nil. It was Wednesday, March 29, 2006, one month and one day since his surgery on Fat Tuesday.

Thursday morning, March 30, Larry's kidney doctor told me with compassion that the doctors had done everything they could have possibly done. The only thing left to do now was to start praying for a miracle. That was exactly what we did. The most difficult thing I ever had to do was tell my children that their father was probably going to die. We began to pray for that miracle when something very special happened.

On Thursday evening, we were all standing around Larry's bed. He had a temperature of 103 degrees. We were praying for that miracle when I noticed a young woman in the hallway trying to get my attention. Loretta, a women from the bank where Larry worked, handed me a card. A picture of a priest was on the front of the card. Imagine my shock as I turned the card over and "The Miracle Prayer" was printed on the back. None of us had ever seen this prayer, and it was just what we needed at that specific time. We read the prayer over Larry. Then Larry's sister took it out to the waiting room, where she and a nurse made twenty copies to pass around the waiting room. It had been decided that everyone would say the prayer every morning at 8:00 AM until Larry had recovered.

By Saturday, Larry's condition worsened and time was running out. If he did not produce white blood cells by Sunday, he would have no chance of survival. A family meeting was set up with the doctors to decide if he should be taken off of life support. It looked as if we were going to have to make those dreaded choices after all on Monday morning.

That Saturday afternoon, our daughter-in-law came into the room and handed me a very old silver cross that opened to reveal a relic of St. Therese of Lisieux, "the little flower of Jesus." A neighbor and friend had brought it to their house and told her that the cross had most likely healed his grandfather some fifty years earlier. Lori pinned the medal with a rosary blessed by the pope to Larry's hospital gown. We prayed it would help.

At this point, Larry's room was beginning to look like a small chapel. Holy cards, scapular medals, and other cards (some made by the grandchildren) covered the bulletin board. One of the side cabinets was being used as a small altar. Statues, prayer books, a bottle of holy water, candles, and several more medals faced Larry's bed in hopes of helping his recovery. Loving friends, priests, and nuns had brought all of these holy artifacts in, and they helped us to keep hoping.

Sadly, the St. Therese relic disappeared the next day and was never recovered. I was so distraught to think that we had lost something so precious and priceless, and it didn't even belong to us. I immediately reported the loss to the charge nurse, and she began an extensive search. I didn't tell my children, because I really felt that it would turn up. Some of the nurses said that the medal was where it needed to be in order to help the next person, but I was still sick about it.

When we told the owners about the loss, they were so very gracious. They said the exact same thing that the nurses had said. Our family still felt terrible that this had happened. I knew I always would, as it was never recovered.

A special bed was ordered for Larry a week or so earlier. This bed rotated to keep fluid from building up in his lungs and around his heart. When we first saw this bed move, it was a frightening sight to see.

Larry had to be tied down to the bed, both hands and feet, because he thrashed nearly the whole time he was in the coma. He seemed to want to get out of bed, and he would have had both feet on the floor if it wasn't for the fact that his feet had been tied down! One of the nurses devised a sling, and by putting pillows inside it, she tried to thwart Larry's attempts to get out of bed. We all thought the days were over of picking one leg up, placing it in bed, and then doing the same with the other leg, but we were wrong. Fifteen minutes later, both feet were back on the floor. We realized right then just how much Larry didn't want to be in that bed. We knew he was trying his hardest to get his life back, but by now, he was so very sick. He needed dialysis badly, because his Creatinine levels were rising at an alarming rate. The kidney doctor told us it would be a death sentence to reinsert the shunt because of the risk of more infection. All we could do now was pray, and that was what all of our friends and dozens of prayer lines were doing.

Larry was slipping away from us, but we kept holding on and hoping. We never gave up. Maybe we were just too stubborn, but our faith was also very strong. We knew God worked miracles, and we knew Larry was trying to come back to us, so we just kept on praying.

*Prayer enlarges the heart until it is capable
of containing God's gift of himself.*
—Mother Theresa

Chapter 3

My Epiphany

It was now Sunday, April 2 and my son, Joe, called me to the waiting room phone to speak with someone. The man on the phone said that this name was Chuck. He continued telling me that I did not know him but that he knew my husband. Chuck told me that Larry had helped him somehow and that God was telling him to go to "the site" to pray for Larry. He asked if it would be all right if he brought some other deacons from the Christian Fellowship Baptist Church to the hospital to pray for Larry. When I said, "Absolutely," Chuck said they would be over around noon.

At exactly noon, the elevator doors opened and out stepped four tall men, all dressed very elegantly. One of the men walked over to me and confirmed that I was Larry's wife. I had told him where I would be sitting. He then told me that they needed to know exactly what to pray for before we went back to Larry's room in the CICU. We then told them that none of us had actually been allowed in the room, because Larry's body was not capable of fighting off infections of any kind; therefore, we would have to stand right outside of his room.

My son and I told them how Larry needed white blood cells most of all if he was to have any chance of recovery. We also told them how every major organ in his body was shutting down and how all the infections were ravaging his body. Now we were ready to proceed to room 929. I told Larry's nurse what we were about to do, and she asked if she could join our prayer circle. Just as she did, all of Larry's machines started going off and ringing, so she had to rush in and tend to Larry during the whole event.

These four men stormed in, taking charge of the prayer. We later found out they referred to themselves as "prayer warriors." That was precisely how we had perceived them that day. They were each so strong and powerful. What happened next changed my life forever.

One of the men started off by reading a scripture. Then each man took his turn praying out loud. They were talking to God as if He were right there with us. They were telling God he needed to place His hands on Larry and all of his healthcare providers. The men called God "the Master Physician," and they knew He healed. And they wanted Him to heal Larry *right now*! They prayed so fervently, and it was so very comforting. I had never seen prayer quite like that. They prayed with urgency and with such confidence. It was very comforting.

While we were praying, I saw what I believed was God slightly elevated over the head of Larry's bed. He was wearing red and white robes, and He had His hand outstretched over Larry. Sparkling, golden, light energy was radiating from His hand and casting onto Larry's body. When I saw this, I had the calmest feeling come over me. I felt at peace for the first time in weeks, and I knew that Larry was going to be fine. That peaceful feeling still has not left me. I now feel like I will always have the strength to handle whatever I am dealt.

After we thanked the gentlemen and they left, I asked my son if he had seen what I had. Joe said that although he had not seen anything—he had had his eyes closed—he had certainly felt something special. My only regret was that my daughter, Annette, had not experienced this feeling as well. She had been three floors down at the time, visiting a sick friend, and she had known nothing about what had happened with our "prayer warriors." I wished she could have been there, for it really had been very moving.

I will not fear for you are ever with me, and you will never leave me to face my perils alone.

—Thomas Merton

CHAPTER 4

TORNADO DRILL

Though unusual in March, we received several weather and tornado warnings for Kansas City in 2006.

One Sunday morning in mid-March, I arrived at the hospital around 5:30 AM. It was storming outside when I went into the CICU and noticed beds with patients scattered around the room. I immediately asked Larry's nurse what had happened. She told me that they had had a tornado warning and had pushed the beds out for safety reasons and covered them with sheets to protect the patients from possible injury from broken glass. Larry's bed was not out there though, and I was concerned. This was called a "code gray."

The nurse explained to me that some patients like Larry could not be moved as they were hooked up to respirators. The best they could do was cover him with a sheet and hope for the best. That was a little unsettling. At least we had survived our first code gray, and all became calm again shortly thereafter.

My daughter, Annette, my granddaughter, Emilee, a family friend of mine, and I had lunch in the cafeteria later that day. I told them all about the code gray and how upset I had been that Larry hadn't been very well protected when the alarm had sounded again.

Another code-gray warning came over the intercom and instructed no one to leave the building and all to go to the safest place in the middle of the building. We headed for the surgery waiting area on the first floor, a safe place with no windows. My granddaughter, Emilee, suddenly burst out and said, "And all they did was throw a sheet over Papa!" I hadn't realized how my earlier remarks had affected this six-year-old girl. She was very upset.

We still were not finished with the code grays; however, after he had been transferred to a step-down room, Larry was awake the next time the alarm sounded. Larry was out of the coma by now, but he still had a lot of drugs in his system, which the doctors were trying to get rid of. Luckily, Larry was still sleeping most of the time.

Late one evening in April after we had gone home, Larry woke up with a sheet over his head. He was scared and started calling for a nurse and asking where he was. One nurse answered right away and said, "Mr. Janacaro, you are out in the hall with the other patients on this floor. There has been a tornado warning. This is a code gray."

Larry later told us that because he was flat on his back with a sheet over him, he had been afraid that the nurses had thought he had died. He said he stared asking for them so that they would know that he wasn't dead. One more code incident happened that last week Larry was in the hospital.

I had left the room to get a cup of coffee from the coffee shop downstairs, and I was on my way back to the room when the sirens started going off. Doors were slammed shut, and people were running down the hallways. When I stopped a nurse to ask her what was happening, she told me that there was a fire somewhere in the hospital and that this was a "code red." Fortunately, there was no fire, but Larry had experienced yet another code. If you are a patient in the hospital long enough, you have the chance to experience all of the codes even if you'd rather not! Whew!

Prayer moves the hand that moves the world.
—John Aikman Wallace

CHAPTER 5

---·•·---

MY DESOLATION

I now understand loneliness, and I have so much more compassion for the lonely people in the world. Loneliness is so quiet. Perhaps too quiet.

When you have had a person around you for over forty years and have shared so much with them, their silence is deafening. "Please talk to me," I often said. "Disagree with me! Anything, just say something!"

Nothing. No response.

I had so many questions I needed to ask Larry when he was in the coma. We had discussed everything all those years and had been through so much together. We had actually been a rather loud and lively family! But all that had shut down as Larry continued to live in a world other than ours, and we were not the same family now. Our core member was not there, our animated, talkative Larry.

Before he checked into the hospital for surgery, Larry had always paid our bills, as he was better at that job than I was. After a month, though, bills came in again, and of course, I needed to take over that responsibility. But I couldn't find the checkbook! My son and I tore Larry's office apart and finally found it. If only we could have asked him. Oh, that deafening silence.

Because I was forced to pay the bills now, I continued to act as the payer for the next several months. Admittedly, I did become quite good at it although Larry was the banker in the family, not me.

As my best friend lay there in a hospital bed, I realized that I had never gone one day since 1966, the year we first started dating, without talking to Larry. That fact was so frustrating and also so very sad. We had always comforted each other through our difficult times, such as the night my mother had passed away. That night, we had laid in bed and had said the rosary together. My comforter couldn't be there this time.

I dreaded going home more than anything. I knew I wasn't there very much, just a few hours to shower and sleep; however, our fun, busy household was nothing like it had once been, and I now had to wonder if Larry would ever walk through the front door again. The longer he was in the hospital, the less likely it seemed that he ever would. I needed him so badly.

The only good part about coming home was that I could let my guard down. After I had gone through the mail, checked phone messages, and such, I could cry, scream, hoping the neighbors didn't hear, and basically have what I liked to call one of my "mini" breakdowns. It seemed to help a little, and then I would pull myself together and try to gather enough strength to go on. I felt I had to be strong for my children and not let them see me cry. Even though my kids were grown and now had children of their own, I felt that showing strength was what I was supposed to do in the situation.

It was hard going home when Larry, with his "bigger than life" personality, was not there, so I would pray when I was alone.

I understood then that it truly was possible to be lonely in a crowd of people. There were so many family members and friends who were there constantly; however, my other half was not, and consequently, I felt so alone. When everyone left to go home and the long hours stretched ahead, I became afraid and asked myself over and over, "How do I do this? How do I make these crucial decisions about Larry's life? What if I'm wrong?" The one person I needed to ask was the one person who needed me to make the right decisions.

And in those lonely moments, I would think about the life we'd had together. We had suffered some terrible losses—the deaths of Larry's dad and mom, my mom, my sister, Larry's baby brother, grandparents, some close friends, and Larry's best guy friend. I had suffered a heart attack in 1999, the same year that Larry had lost his right kidney to cancer. But we had survived and had some wonderful times with our children and grandchildren. I loved our life, and now it looked to be over. I didn't want it to be finished. It was such a great life.

As I spoke of this to one of the wise nurses, she said that I was mourning the loss of our married life. And I was. She was right.

Sometimes I would just sit in the hospital chapel. It was quiet in there, and I could actually attempt to get my thoughts in order. It was during one of these times that I realized I really wasn't alone. God was with me and always had been at every step of the way. These visits always made me feel a little better and a little stronger. I knew I could not give up. Somehow, I would cope.

One day, a male nurse turned the radio on to a country-western music station, because I had told him that was the kind of music Larry liked. I was standing by Larry's bed and wiping his forehead, because he had a 104 degree temperature, when the song "Stand By Your Man" came on. Tears streamed down my face, because I knew that was exactly what I was doing. The song only encouraged me to keep it up. I knew that if the roles had been reversed, Larry would have stood by me no matter what.

Janacaro Family

Larry

Patti

Faith is to believe what you do not yet see: The reward of this faith is to see what you believe.

—Saint Augustine

Chapter 6

The Miracle

On Sunday, April 2, Larry finally got the white blood cells he so desperately needed at the last minute. If he had not gotten the blood cells that day, we would have had to decide whether to keep him on life support or not. It must have been the combination of all the prayer chains, the Miracle Prayer, the relic of St. Therese, the "prayer warriors," the prayers of all of the priests and nuns who had come daily to pray for him, and our faith that brought this miracle to us. It had definitely been the power of prayer that had helped him.

The prayers I had prayed every night as a little girl of seven years old had been answered. I had prayed to God that I could witness a miracle like St. Bernadette. I wanted that so badly. Even though it had taken fifty years, what better miracle could I have witnessed than that of my husband's recovery?

We began to smile again on Monday morning as Larry's doctor told us how rapidly he was improving. Everything was returning to normal after a month filled with so many medical procedures, close encounters with death, and so much grief and sadness.

Now it was time to begin waking Larry up. We needed to get him up and moving, because all of his muscles had atrophied from being in bed for such a long time. He could not sit up or walk without assistance. After he had been on so many drugs for such a long time, he didn't actually wake up for two full weeks after his recovery. It was Holy Saturday, and Father Waris, our pastor, walked into Larry's step-down room. Father took one look at Larry and said, "This is proof of the resurrection right here." Father Waris told Larry's story at Easter Sunday's mass that year.

CHAPTER 7

ICU PSYCHOSIS

ICU psychosis is something we were not at all prepared for, and it was one of the hardest issues we had to deal with throughout this whole ordeal. During this time, he was nothing like our former Larry.

When he started waking up, he felt like he was being held captive. We were all wearing masks because of the infections he had just endured. He did not know where he was, for he did not remember coding that first time on March 3, which had ultimately brought him to the CICU. He was totally confused.

Larry was shocked when he found out how much time had passed and how much he had missed out on. He wanted to catch up immediately and became quite agitated when we could not supply information quickly enough.

Communication was slow, and Larry could not speak yet because of the tracheotomy tube. He had to try to write his feelings on paper. Because of all the drugs and the lack of use of his hands, his writing was unrecognizable. We couldn't figure out what he was trying to tell us. He became extremely irritated and angry. Finally, one day, I looked at what he had scratched on the paper and realized it said, "Escape." He wanted me to help him escape from the hospital. He showed this to several friends and some nurses. They all told him, "No, you can't leave until you are better." Larry was becoming frustrated and uncontrollable, trying to get out of the bed whenever he wanted. A safe measure was installed in his bed so that whenever he attempted to get out of bed, an alarm would ring, and the nurses would rush in, because he could not stand on his own yet.

Larry kept pleading with me to help him escape. Everyone was telling him *no*. I decided that maybe what he needed was a little hope. Maybe he would calm down if he had some hope.

I eventually leaned down and got really close to his ear so that no one could hear what I was going to say. I told him that I would help him escape when the coast was clear but that this had to be our little secret. He looked up at me with such gratitude, and he really seemed to feel a little less trapped. For several days, he asked me when we were alone if now was the time. I would walk out to the hallway, look both ways, walk back into his room, and tell him, "Not yet." I would then tell him that as soon as both corridors were free of nurses, we would go. All he needed was a little hope. Didn't we all?

Soon, the psychosis faded, and he began to return to his old self. This was cause for real celebration!

If the only prayer you say in your whole life
is thank you that would suffice.

—Meister Eckhart

Chapter 8

Newspapers

Before Larry had checked into the hospital, he had made me promise to save the daily newspaper and the *Wall Street Journal* for him. He hadn't wanted to miss anything during the three to four days he had been scheduled to stay in the hospital after his kidney surgery. Because he had always read the paper from cover to cover every day, this was very important to him.

Therefore, every morning before I left for the hospital, I would go outside, pick up the paper, and throw it in the backseat of my car. Every night, I would pick up the *Wall Street Journal* and do the same thing.

Well, after a couple of weeks, the backseat started to get pretty full. The three or four days had turned into weeks and then a month. Finally, it had been two and a half months, and I was still performing my daily ritual.

After we had been home a while, I asked Larry if he wanted me to bring in the papers for him to read, explaining that I had saved every one of them. He looked at me like I was crazy, and he couldn't believe that I had saved every single one. Then he told me that there was no way that he could possibly read all of those papers.

After I left the room and rolled my eyes as I usually did, I went to the car, drove to the St. Patrick's parking lot, and deposited all of the papers in the recycling bin. Perhaps I had taken his request a little too literally.

I am happy that the church benefited from my actions, though, and it was pretty comical as we had watched the backseat fill up with papers.

CHAPTER 9

AFTER THE MIRACLE

I t took at least two full weeks for Larry to completely wake up. We were told that this was not unusual for someone who had been in a coma for six weeks.

Larry stayed in the CICU for only a week after he had come out of the coma. The doctors were very pleased at the speed of his recovery. Eventually, the time came to move him to a step-down room, something that earlier we had feared would never happen. Larry, who had been the most critical patient in the CICU, was now too well to stay in the unit. Unbelievable! We were a little frightened by his move out of the comfortable room with the nurses and their skills at his disposal. They helped bring him back to us. We knew, however; that this was a huge step in his recovery. A new chapter had begun.

Chapter 10

The Recovery

Larry's rapid recovery amazed the doctors. They came by to check on the "Miracle Man," as they had named him, and told us they had never seen anyone as sick as he had been recover. One of the doctors told us that he had never believed in miracles until that moment.

We would try to explain all that had happened to Larry as he was coming off the drugs. It was a slow process. Until they were able to remove the tracheotomy tube, he still had to write to communicate with us. His muscles were so weak that he could hardly hold a pen.

We also needed to update him on what had been going on in the world while he had "slept" for six weeks.

Thankfully, there was no cognitive damage to his brain. Larry had always been a historian and trivia buff, and the doctors had been worried that being in a coma for so long might have affected him somehow. However, absolutely no damage occurred, and Larry was still as sharp as a tack.

When Larry's sister, Nola, asked if he had seen a light or anything like that, Larry told her that he remembered only one thing. He said he didn't know when the moment had occurred exactly. He said, "First, I smelled the cologne Old Spice that dad had worn. Then I saw a man in work clothes with his back to me. The man then turned around, and he was very angry with me. He told me to get out of there; I didn't belong in there, to go back." Larry's dad had passed away forty years earlier.

Larry was in the step-down room for a week before he was moved to the physical rehabilitation unit. After intense physical rehab twice a day for a week and a half, the doctors said he could finally come home.

Fifty pounds lighter, Larry left the hospital with his children and four grandchildren on May 3 with the help of a walker and a cane. He spent the next six weeks in and out of physical therapy sessions. He soon needed neither the cane nor the walker.

After three months, we both returned to work in June. The only side effect was numbness in his hand from being tied down for six weeks. Now, even that is gone, too! Larry has completely recovered. To look at him, you would never imagine that he had spent two and a half months in the hospital with such serious complications. While on vacation in October, he rode a bicycle ten miles each day. Before the surgery, Larry took four medications daily plus an aspirin. Now, Larry takes only the ten milligrams of Inderal for migraines, a prescription that he has taken for thirty years now.

When Larry went in for his three-month checkup, the doctor told him that his one remaining partial kidney had actually grown a little bit. This didn't usually happen. At

Larry's dental checkup, the staff was amazed at the condition of this teeth and gums. They were even better than before. Usually, when someone took so many drugs and breathed through a respirator for such a long period of time, a lot of damage occurred. This was not so in Larry's case.

The whole ordeal took place between Fat Tuesday and Easter Sunday. This truly was a Lenten miracle. We now have proof that miracles still happen in today's modern world. Prayer brought our miracle to us. It's the power of prayer. Yeah, that's power!